Using

Radar

Other titles of interest

Using GPS, 2nd ed.
Conrad Dixon
Using GPS aims to help owners get the best from their sets and make full use of the facilities available, whether simply position fixing and course setting or interfacing with integrated navigation systems. Seven sets are compared function by function.

Basic Coastal Navigation, 2nd ed.
Frank J. Larkin
A clearly written, easy to understand introduction to coastal navigation, outlining fundamental techniques for safe navigation in small boats under power or sail. Each chapter includes practice scenarios of increasing difficulty, making this book an excellent self-teaching guide.

Quick & Easy Guide to Compass Correction
George H. Reid
This guide provides all the information required to determine a ship's compass error, its true course and how to adjust the compass. It gives step-by-step instructions on how to swing ship, set up deviation tables and adjust compasses.

Celestial Navigation in a Nutshell
Hewitt Schlereth
Even in the age of technology, celestial navigation is still an essential method of plotting one's course. This guide explains clearly and concisely how to navigate any stretch of sea using only a few traditional navigation tools. Several examples and situational illustrations are included throughout.

How to Choose Your First Powerboat
Chuck Gould
Buying a powerboat is one of the biggest financial commitments a boater can make. This book covers the basics of what to look for in a new powerboat, from comfort and cost to inspecting the engine, fuel and electrical systems, and taking the boat for a sea trial.

Sheridan House Inc.
www.sheridanhouse.com

Using
Radar

A practical guide for small craft

Robert Avis

S

SHERIDAN HOUSE

To my very best friend,
who now knows far more about radar
than she ever really wanted to know!

Published 2000 by
Sheridan House Inc
145 Palisade Street
Dobbs Ferry
NY 10522

www.sheridanhouse.com

Library of Congress Cataloging-in-Publication Data

Avis, Robert
  Using radar; a practical guide for small craft/Robert
  Avis.
    p. cm.
  Includes index.
  ISBN 1-57409-105-0
    1. Radar in navigation. 2. Boats and boating—Radar
  equipment. I. Title.

VK560 . A86 2000
623.89′33—dc21   99-056900

Printed in Great Britain

Contents

Acknowledgements

My sincere thanks to the following people and organisations who have been enormously helpful in compiling and checking the information in this book:

Harry Cook MBE MNI
Furuno UK Ltd
Raytheon Marine Company
Tolley Marine Ltd
Sea Start
RAMAR Sea Training Radar Course, HMS Dryad

1 • Why Choose Radar?

It is difficult to imagine just how different our lives would be today without radar. Without realising it, radar technology has a hand in so many of our everyday activities. It provides the weatherman with a basis upon which to forecast; helps the police to encourage us to observe the speed limit; automatically opens supermarket doors as we approach with our laden shopping trolleys; it enables space scientists to map out faraway planets; and it turns on the outside light at the approach of an unexpected visitor; and ... oh, by the way, it is a *brilliant* aid to navigators the world over!

Just cast an eye over virtually every merchant ship or warship as they pass and you will spot their rotating radar scanners. Professional seamen, trained in the use of radar, know its value when it comes to collision avoidance, pilotage and coastal navigation. But for some inexplicable reason, radar is still not widely accepted as a navigation aid by sailing folk; perhaps it is the idea that the sets use too much power or that they are difficult to adjust and interpret.

However, attitudes are changing and now, with the introduction of a Royal Yachting Association approved one-day radar course, sailors have the ideal opportunity to find out just how useful radar can be as a navigation aid. If you are considering buying a radar, the course also provides a good forum for asking all the questions you may have.

I personally would save up for a radar set long before buying a GPS, plotter or any other electronic nav-aid.

Why? Well let me tell you a salutary tale. I was invigilating at a Yachtmaster examination a year or so ago, and one of my two candidates was conducting a navigation exercise heading westwards on a coastal passage. He had chosen to pass safely to the north of a well-known shingle bank when that ill-disciplined fender and bucket 'slipped and fell' overboard.

The shout of 'For exercise, Man Overboard!' alerted our skipper and the boat was thrown into a Williamson turn which the candidate considered appropriate as his crew prepared for the recovery. The flybridge motor yacht which we were using only had one satisfactory recovery point and that was on the bathing platform aft. We were soon approaching the casualty and stopped perfectly - just as it says in textbooks. We lay gently just off the bucket and, using a long boat hook, the casualty was eased gently towards the bathing platform whereupon I asked the candidate (six feet tall and rather skinny) to imagine that his colleague, the other candidate (five feet tall and wide, and about 350lb in weight), was in the water. What was he going to do? After putting his mind through some desperate mental hoops, he replied hesitantly that it would depend whether he considered that the casualty was in grave and imminent danger ... if so, he would make a MAYDAY broadcast. This was the answer I might have expected.

We looked over the transom to see the fender bobbing dangerously underneath the bathing platform as we rolled around in the gentle swell. We both came to the conclusion that the candidate would most definitely have been in trouble as there was no way that the casualty could have been lifted out by one person (examiners are not supposed to get involved unless their personal safety comes into question).

Continuing with the exam, I asked the candidate to write down the message he would send, but made it quite clear that he should not, *repeat not*, send it. After some frantic scribbling he came up with his answer. It was perfect in every respect except, perhaps, that he had decided to take our position from the GPS in latitude and longitude. Now, I have a bee in my bonnet that only people in the middle of nowhere (do you remember Tony Bullimore who capsized in the Southern Ocean?) should give their position in lat and long as it doesn't paint any sort of picture to potential rescuers as to where help is needed. What was even more worrying was that, at the precise second that he looked at the GPS, it led us quite confidently to believe that we were some 37 nautical miles away! If only my man had looked at his radar, which had been switched on but left in the standby mode since leaving port, he would have seen without much difficulty that we were three miles north of an extremely well-known landmark which would have been very much more helpful to anyone listening.

Anyway, he didn't refer to his radar, and, perhaps more worryingly, nor did he notice that the GPS was talking complete hogwash. I gave him three more opportunities to review our position, but he stuck religiously to the spurious GPS read-out. Needless to say, we didn't bother going on with his exam. About 10 minutes later, the GPS was back to its normal accuracy of about 200 metres. Sometimes life can be really unfair, can't it?

The moral of the story is to make sure that all your nav equipment is telling you the same story before reaching any firm conclusions. If something doesn't agree, then make sure that you concentrate on the real live information: the type that you get from a radar. You might misinterpret the picture if you're not very experienced, but one thing is for sure, it will not show you things that aren't there.

2 • *The Basic Principles*

HISTORY

The word **RADAR** derives from **RA**dio **D**irection **A**nd **R**anging. It describes the principle of using extremely high frequency radio waves to detect solid objects. It was Heinrich Rudolph Hertz, in 1886, who proved conclusively that radio waves could be reflected. Another German, Christian Hülsmeyer from Düsseldorf, had his British Patent for a 'Hertzian Wave Projecting and Receiving Apparatus ...' approved in London in 1904. Marconi was promoting the feasibility of such equipment for use in ships in 1922, but the real breakthrough came during 1938. In the turbulent days before the start of World War II, government money was poured into research into radio waves, as the technology was considered of crucial importance in the war effort.

RADIO WAVES

The whole concept of radar technology has grown from discoveries in the middle of the nineteenth century that extremely high frequency radio waves (often referred to as microwaves), like light, travel in straight lines and are reflected when they come into contact with solid objects. The challenge for radar pioneers was to design a device that could fire a pulse of microwaves in a predetermined direction and catch any reflected echoes, whilst measuring the time they had taken since they left the transmitter. The speed of a pulse of microwaves had been measured at just under 162,000 nautical miles (nm) per second. (To put this in perspective, a pulse could travel to the moon and back in just over 2½ seconds.)

So if the time a microwave pulse took to return could be measured, then a simple equation: *Distance = speed x time* could be used to determine twice the distance to an object, because the radio waves would need to travel both there and back. By halving the distance, the correct range of a target could then be established.

For example, if we were to send off a pulse of microwaves at time *t1* and they returned at time *t2*. We could calculate

that, because of the known speed at which radio waves travel, the total distance they travelled would be *162,000 x (t2 − t1)*. This answer in nautical miles then has to be halved (because the microwaves have had to go there and back) to give the distance between the transmitter/receiver and the target.

This established that radar could be used to determine range, but all sorts of problems arose when the pioneers discovered that very short pulses did not contain much power and were only effective at short range. Longer, more powerful pulses were required to travel longer distances. At the same time they found that the returns from one pulse had to be received before the next was sent off, otherwise the interference would thoroughly confuse the operator. So, the longer the pulse, the longer the interval between pulses.

TRANSMITTING & RECEIVING   On a modern yacht radar set the time delay between the start of each pulse varies with the range setting as shown below.
(A microsecond (μs) is one millionth of a second)

Operating range	Length of pulse	Pulse cycle
Short range, say up to 1nm	0.08μs	444μs
Medium range, say 1nm − 6nm	0.35μs	667μs
Longer range, say 6nm − 24nm	0.70μs	1,333μs
Long range, say 24nm or more	1.20μs	2,000μs

As can be seen, the length of each pulse is only a tiny fraction of the complete pulse cycle. When your radar says its peak power is rated at, say 2kW or 4kW or even up to 10kW or more, don't worry, it only requires this for barely half a per cent of the time it is actually operating. In more realistic terms, a medium-sized yacht radar will only require between 30 and 55 watts from a 12 or 24 volt supply. More sophisticated models seen on superyachts use 50 to 200 watts.

PULSE REPETITION FREQUENCY

The pulse cycle or more correctly pulse repetition interval (PRI) is normally quoted in the number of cycles it completes per second which is known as the pulse repetition frequency (PRF) and measured in Hertz (Hz); so we can revise the table above to show the PRF as follows.

Operating range	Length of pulse	Pulse cycle
Short range, say up to 1nm	0.08µs	2,250 Hz
Medium range, say 1nm – 6nm	0.35µs	1,500 Hz
Longer range, say 6nm – 24nm	0.70µs	750 Hz
Long range, say 24nm or more	1.20µs	500 Hz

RADAR RANGES

The maximum range of a radar is determined not so much by the amount of power you pump into it as by the distance that it can actually 'see'. As with light, there is a limit to the distance we can see which, at sea, we call the horizon. But there is a difference between the optical horizon (OH), the distance we can actually see, and the radar horizon (RH), the distance a radar can see.

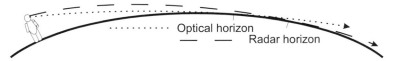

Although we suppose that light and microwaves travel in a straight line, they both get refracted (slightly bent) towards the earth by the earth's atmosphere.

The optical horizon (OH) in nautical miles is calculated:
2.08 x √height of eye in metres

The radar horizon (RH) in nautical miles is calculated:
2.23 x √height of radar antenna in metres

The radar horizon is slightly further away than the optical horizon because microwaves are refracted slightly more by the earth's atmosphere than light. I suppose this makes radar technically more effective as a navigation aid than the mark-one eyeball, but I think I'll still stick to my tried and tested eyes, leaving the radar close behind as number two!

Now, these figures are all very well, but they assume that you are looking for a horizon. We all know that radar isn't going to see a horizon, because there isn't anything there to see. So how can we calculate the range at which a radar might pick up, say some distant cliffs?

Radar horizon

The effective radar range in nautical miles is calculated using heights in metres as follows:

2.23 x (√antenna height + √cliff height)

This would account in part for my being able to pick up the rock of Gibraltar some 92 miles away on a 48nm Furuno radar set (using the offset centre feature) in a 20m motor yacht with an antenna height of 6m. If this subject fascinates you, read Chapter 5 which includes super-refraction and ducting, both of which also considerably extend the normally expected range of radar sets.

BEAM WIDTH

So far we have discovered how a radar can be used to measure distance. It can also, though less precisely, be used to measure bearings. By rotating the radar antenna at a fixed rate (usually around 20–24 times per minute for most small-craft sets) each pulse will have plenty of time to get out to its required range, and if reflected, get back before the antenna has rotated any appreciable amount. If the direction of the antenna can be precisely controlled, the direction from which the returning echoes come can be identified. However, there is a problem because a pulse of microwaves is not sharp or flat like a knife edge. It has a height and a width. The height is known as the *vertical beam width*. The vertical beam width is around 25°–30° which is large enough to compensate for the rolling or pitching of the boat.

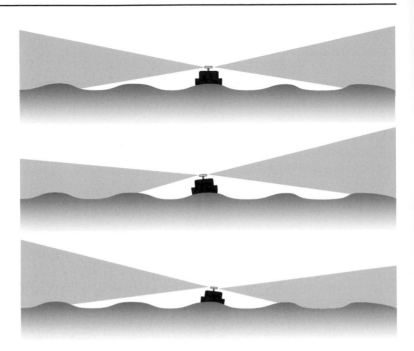

Vertical beam width.

The *horizontal beam width* varies from set to set, but on a small-craft radar set it is normally between 1.2°–6°. This means that any bearing you take needs to be used with a certain amount of caution.

The horizontal beam width determines the clarity of the image on the radar set. A narrow beam will be able to differentiate between two objects that are close together; a wide beam will not.

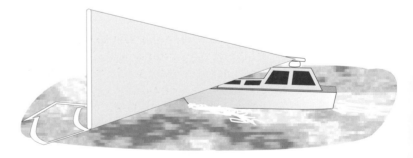

The whole microwave beam is tall and very slim.

It is a proven fact that the width of the beam produced by a radar antenna is inversely proportional to the width of the antenna. Therefore the wider the radar antenna, the narrower

the width of the beam. It is not until you get up to merchant
– and warship – sized antennae that the horizontal beam
width can be reduced to much less than 1°. Hence you will
find that smaller radar antennae, many of which are enclosed
inside a radome or protective cover (see page 17), will have
the widest horizontal beam widths of up to 6°. A 4ft wide
(non-enclosed) antenna, often referred to as an 'open array
antenna', might be rated at, say 2° whilst a 6ft model would
probably be down to a little over 1°. These are factors to
consider when contemplating the purchase of a new radar
set, as they will make a difference to your ability to take accurate bearings.

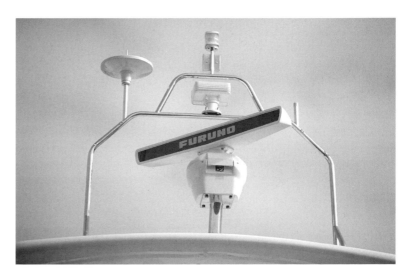

*The wider the
radar antenna, the
narrower the beam,
giving better
definition of
objects.*

THE SCREEN   Radar screens come in a variety of formats and shapes. The
traditional circular screen has slowly given way to square
and oblong versions. It is also possible to customise the
screen to show a host of information produced by electronic
navigation aids. But remember that every piece of extra
information you display on the screen may distract you from
the most important information a radar can give you: a real-
time 'picture' of the surrounding area. The important thing
to note is that radar will only display the return echoes of
solid objects which were actually there within the past three
seconds and are, therefore, almost certainly still there!

Radar antennae rotate 20–24 times per minute so the picture will be updated every 2½–3 seconds; more than adequate in most circumstances. However, if you are in a boat travelling at 25 knots and you meet, head on, a fast ferry at say 40 knots, the combined closing speed of 65 knots will mean that, if first detected on the edge of the three-mile range, you will have less than three minutes before you pass each other. You will close on each other by 110 yards for each sweep of the radar antenna! This may give a strange effect on the radar screen, so take great care if you cruise where fast vessels operate.

Radar screens come in many different shapes and sizes, so there will be one to suit your boat. Boat shows are good places to make comparisons and see demonstrations.

Until the mid 1980s, the radar screen was generally a fluorescent-coated circular glass plate, onto which a beam of electrons was projected. If a solid object reflected the microwaves back to the receiver, this in turn excited an electron beam, causing the fluorescent surface to react and change colour, thus providing the picture. The advantage with this type of analogue display was that the picture was very clear and, as the fluorescent surface maintained its colour for a few

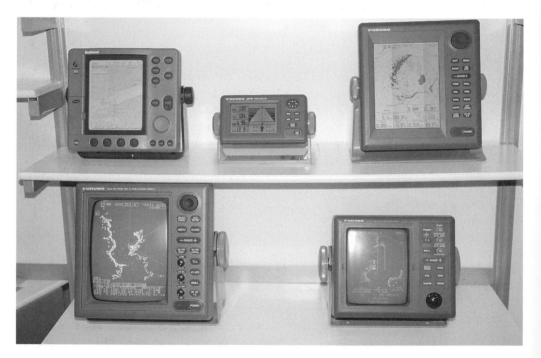

seconds before it faded away, it gave the operator time to interpret the picture before the next sweep of the electron beam updated the image. The disadvantage, however, was that it was nigh on impossible to see with any clarity in daylight without pressing your eyes against a face-shaped slit in a large black rubber hood. Continually alternating between looking at daylight and then peering at the dark screen was very tiring on the eyes.

Large pixels.   *Smaller pixels.*

The mid 1980s saw the introduction of a new type of screen made up of thousands and thousands of tiny pixels activated individually in the same way as the picture on a computer screen is compiled. The early and the less expensive models had very grainy pictures as the pixels were relatively large and therefore difficult to make into a smooth picture. As technology has progressed, the picture quality has improved dramatically and the great advantage is that modern digital screens can be seen in daylight. They come in two types:

Cathode ray tube display (CRT) which is usually a brightly coloured image against a black background.
Liquid crystal display (LCD) which generally displays a dark grey image against a lighter grey background.

Of the two, the CRT display tends to be more bulky and uses more power than the LCD but gives very crisp pictures.
As technology has progressed, not only have the pixels

become much smaller but also some models have what are called quantized pixels. Their colour can be graduated from light to dark giving an even smoother picture than before.

Some LCD screens have the option of reversing the light grey and dark grey for use at night, so that the dark becomes light and vice versa. This is to cut down the bright glare and allow safer night

Typical LCD display.

On the left is an LCD screen that gives a lighter image than the CRT type (right) but has the advantage of not being so bulky and using less power.

vision. However, the CRT screen, by using different colours to show different strengths of signal, is more easily understood by the less experienced eye. Despite its strengths, for the moment the considerable additional cost of a colour screen would not tempt me to buy one. No doubt as technology races on, it won't be too long before colour becomes the standard option.

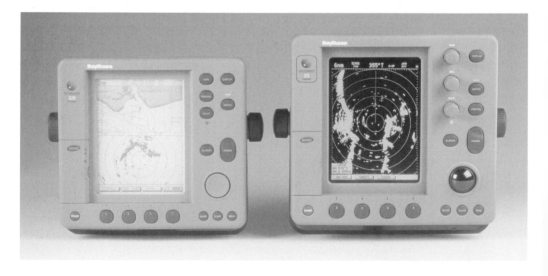

POSITIONING THE ANTENNA AND DISPLAY

Perhaps the most important aspect of installing a radar is to get the antenna or aerial in the optimum position. We have seen that the height at which the antenna is installed will affect its range capabilities, but you must also bear in mind that if you go for the ultimate position at the top of the mast, then any rolling, pitching or continuous heeling will seriously affect its 'view'. Also, additional weight will be placed at the top of the mast. Radomes, the enclosed antennae, start at around 4kg in weight. The larger, open array antennae can be as much as 30kg and more. It is important to ensure that if the unit is to be mast-mounted, the rigging supporting the mast is strong enough for the job. Sailing boats should ensure that running rigging cannot become entangled in rotating open array antennae. As an alternative to mounting the antenna on the mast, a special 'mast', about 2–3 metres high is often mounted right aft near the transom. This keeps the antenna well clear of unwanted rigging.

Before deciding finally, check out the all-round view. Are there masts, funnel(s) crosstrees, chimneys or other obstructions in the way? Exhaust smoke from a funnel should be kept well clear as the inevitable sooty deposits will soon degrade the efficiency of the antenna as will continuous temperatures above about 70°C which may be encountered near an exhaust outlet.

Radome mounted on the mizzen mast

Radome mounted on the main mast

Radome mounted on special 'mast' aft keeps it clear of rigging

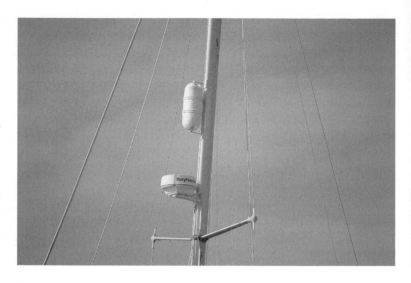

Make sure that your antenna – in this case enclosed in a radome – is not too heavy for its location on the mast and that it is unlikely to obstruct the rigging.

The next consideration is the signal cable that connects the antenna to the radar display unit. Manufacturers do not recommend runs of cable in excess of 30m – plenty for the average yacht or motor cruiser. The cable run should be kept as short as possible and without any joins. The signal cable

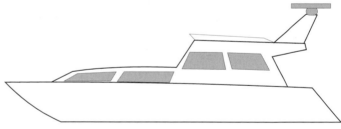

Radar antenna (or radome) mounted above flybridge.

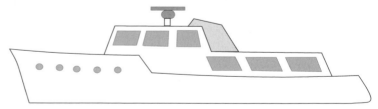

Radar antenna raised above obstruction.

This radome is mounted on its own support, clear of rigging and any obstructions which may block the transmission and reception of microwaves.

may have as many as twenty individual leads enclosed inside it and it will be shielded. Nevertheless, it is not good practice to run the cable parallel to other electrical wiring in the boat, as interference between the cables may cause operational problems.

The positioning of the radar display unit is equally important. It must be comfortable to use. If you decide to fit it to a deck beam, make sure that you will not get a crick in your neck looking at it. Similarly, if you decide to install the screen inside the cabin, make sure it can be seen from the helm. If you are a single-handed sailor there is no point in installing it where you will never get a chance to see it!

Should the screen be forward-facing? Current international regulations insist on a forward-facing radar. Whilst there are no such obligations put upon amateurs, it is important to ask yourself if you are someone who can easily orientate yourself to understand the picture, no matter which way you and the screen are pointing.

If you have decided that **HEAD-UP** mode is for you (see Chapter 6 on screen orientation), you may find it easier to understand the picture if the display is forward-facing with the radar picture facing the same way as you are travelling. If you are a convert to **NORTH-UP** mode, which I certainly am, then it is probably not so important. The screen's position relative to direct sunlight should be considered. Even 'daylight' sets will not be at their best when challenged by a direct beam of bright sunlight.

It is important that you check the safe distance between the radar display unit and your magnetic steering compass. Usually this is between 0.5m–1.2m but details will be found in the instructions supplied with the radar.

INSTALL IT YOURSELF?

The biggest decision, having decided upon a radar, is who is going to fit it. If you were to read your manufacturer's instruction book, it would appear that nothing could be simpler. Unfortunately this may not be the case. Although connecting up the set is relatively straightforward, the peripheral work – running the cables and ensuring that cable runs are not interfering with, or being interfered with by, other electrical installations – can be problematical. Then there is the cosmetic problem of concealing the cables and mounting the radar display unit. Is it to be mounted in its own bracket on a horizontal surface, or on a vertical surface, or is it to be flush-mounted into a console? If you are going to flush-mount it, make sure there is sufficient space around the back – do not forget that radar sets get warm whilst they are operating and require a circulation of air around them. Do not be tempted to cut the cables too short. You should allow a long service loop on each cable behind the set so that any maintenance can be carried out without being constrained by short cables.

The set will need to be grounded between the ground terminal on the display unit and the vessel's earthing plate. It is

This series of photos shows the installation of a radome on the radar arch of a motor boat. **Top left:** *fastening the radome to the supporting structure; you can see the antenna mounted inside.* **Right:** *the weatherproof cover is being set in place.* **Bottom left:** *make sure you leave a long service loop of cable behind the installation. If you do your own installation (bottom right) you will find that you need the agility of a ferret!*

worth finding out where the earthing plate is fitted when planning the installation. If your set is designed to operate with either 12 volt or 24 volt supply, it may be necessary to change the main fuse in the power cable from 10 amps for 12 volts to 5 amps for 24 volts. It is important to check this with the installation instructions before switching on for the first time in order to protect the set.

The installation routine is vitally important to the satisfactory use of the radar. You will be required to adjust the tune and video amplifier. The radar needs to know the height of the antenna. The heading marker can be adjusted so that a contact dead ahead of you is dead ahead on the display. The sweep timing must be adjusted to account for the time the trigger pulse takes to get from the display unit to the antenna to trigger off the transmitter. With a little care and patience, all these tasks can be achieved by the uninitiated, but you should remember that they are all vital to the efficient operation of the radar set.

So, do you feel confident to tackle installation? If you do you will have to be a very able joiner, electrician, contortionist and project manager. There is a risk that even when you think you have followed the installation instructions religiously, for some inexplicable reason, the radar still won't work. Inevitably, it is not the unit which is at fault but some really simple error which you cannot detect.

Installation instructions are, by their very nature, written by people who know how the installation should be done, and with a depth of experience behind them that few of us lesser mortals will ever have. Therefore it has to be accepted that the amateur starts off at a great disadvantage. If you do decide to go it alone, for goodness sake, don't cut any cables or fix anything down finally until you are confident that it is all working correctly. This is most definitely a job where you first should study the fitting instructions carefully and not just look at the book once you meet a snag.

You've probably gathered by now that having saved up for the set, I personally would spend that little bit more on the services of a professional to install it. This avoids arguments about warranties and how it got broken.

Once the set is installed and working satisfactorily, it will almost certainly be necessary to have the steering compass re-swung to ensure that the installation of the radar has not markedly affected the boat's deviation. To ensure accuracy, the compass must be re-swung while all the electrical equipment that is normally in use during a passage is operating.

A WORD OF CAUTION

If you are buying a selection of electronic navigation equipment from different manufacturers and having it installed together, do not assume that, because each item claims to support the international standard for marine electronics NMEA 0183, you will automatically be able to pass the information provided between all the equipment you have fitted. Different manufacturers use different internal electronic languages. Unless your equipment is made by the same manufacturer, using the same electronic language, it is quite likely that, although latitude and longitude information will travel freely, depth, wind, heading and time information may not transfer without special adaptation. Most of us amateurs do not consider this at the time of purchase, nor do we warm to the additional costs which are inevitably involved.

When you are specifying navigation equipment, be absolutely sure in your own mind what you are expecting each piece of equipment to do. This is important if you wish to avoid disappointment later.

The radar takes centre stage in this handsome walnut dashboard.

OFF/STANDBY/
TRANSMIT
(TX)

At last the magic moment arrives when you turn on your radar set for the first time. If you have the open array type of antenna (ie it is not concealed inside a radome or rigid cover) first of all check that there is nothing tangled around the antenna or able to become tangled Sod's Law says that if you have any loose running rigging, it will inevitably find a way of snagging an open array radar antenna.

Radar has three stages of activity: **OFF** which is self-explanatory; **STANDBY** which indicates that the radar is going through a preparatory sequence or it is ready for action but not actually transmitting any pulses from the antenna; and **TRANSMIT** which indicates that it is literally 'burning and turning'.

Radar sets take a while to warm up when you first turn them on. The magnetron, which triggers off the microwave pulses that enable the radar to function at all, needs to be at its correct operating temperature before it can run effectively. When the set is first switched from **OFF** to **STANDBY**, it will take between 90 seconds and three minutes to warm up. Most sets go through a countdown phase which appears on the screen to let you know how the warming-up procedure is progressing. Once the magnetron has reached its operating temperature, pressing the **TX** or **TRANSMIT** button will activate the system. The antenna will start to rotate and the magnetron will begin sending out pulses of microwaves. This is by no means the end of the switching on procedure. The most important part follows. If the set is not correctly set up initially it will be next to useless, so the correct adjustment of the *brilliance, gain, range* and *tuning* is absolutely vital.

BRILLIANCE

BRILLIANCE control adjusts the overall brightness of the screen: it will need to be turned down in darkness and turned up in daylight. This requires very little skill on the part of the operator. If you cannot see the screen, turn up the **BRILLIANCE** and vice versa.

GAIN

The **GAIN** is more important as it controls the amplification applied to returning echoes. If the gain is set too low, many small contacts may be lost, and if turned up too high, the screen will be covered in tiny speckles obscuring smaller echoes. These are caused by inter-ference known as *radio noise*. The optimum setting is when the speckles are just on the cusp of appearing or disappearing.

Gain set too high.

RANGE

The **RANGE** control makes the radar versatile. It can operate at very close range (down to ¼nm or even ⅛nm) and its range can be increased in stages up to 12, 16, 24, 48 and even 72 nautical miles or more (on the larger more powerful and more power-consuming sets).

There are two things to consider about the range when set-ting up the set. First, there must be a potential radar contact within range to tune the set to. This may sound obvious, but just consider for a moment that you have started off on an offshore passage and you have the radar turned off. Halfway along, you run into a bank of fog. On goes the radar but if there are no radar contacts within range, you cannot tune the set in effectively. It will be hit and miss as to whether you really can use it with any confidence. Secondly, the ideal range for setting up and tuning in is somewhere between three and six miles so you are dependent upon a good strong contact within that range.

TUNING

TUNING is absolutely vital to the effectiveness of the radar. The radar receiver must be adjusted precisely to receive the maximum number of reflections from the surrounding contacts. As a rule of thumb, the optimum position for the tuning knob is likely to be between one-third and one-half of the way around its entire scope. It certainly does not follow that the higher you set the tuning, the better tuned the set will be. Try to find a contact on the outer limits of the range selected and tune the set to get the optimum image. It may take a couple of minutes or so to find it, but don't rush the tuning stage or the whole setting up procedure may be compromised.

To help the inexperienced, many radar sets are fitted with a *tuning indicator* (see right), whereby the more boxes that are filled, the better the set is tuned.

You may find that each time you change scale, you need to retune the radar for the best results. This may seem tedious but the quality of the picture will make it worth the effort.

AUTOMATIC TUNING

If you are still bemused by the whole concept of tuning, do not give up hope, as modern sets invariably have an optional *automatic tuning* facility which will monitor and adjust the optimum tuning setting for you, not only when you switch on but also when you change range.

SETTING UP

If you are very observant, you may have noticed that the correct order of setting up the radar controls is:

BRILLIANCE – GAIN – RANGE – TUNING

which is conveniently in alphabetical order. Remembering this is helpful when determining the order in which you should set up a radar for the optimum image.

There are a number of ways that the screen can be made easier to understand, and removing *clutter* is one of the most important.

SEA CLUTTER

SEA CLUTTER (see above right) is one of the most frustrating problems. Because of the wide vertical beam width (normally about 25°–30°) the pulses of micro-waves are highly susceptible to reflection from waves in the close vicinity of the boat, particularly if it is rolling around in a swell. This causes the image to be confused around the centre of the screen. This sea clutter can be reduced or even removed by utilising the **ANTI-CLUTTER (SEA)** or **SEA CLUTTER** control. However ...

Sea clutter.

**THE ANTI-CLUTTER (SEA) CONTROL MUST
BE USED WITH EXTREME CAUTION.**

It is very easy to remove not only the sea clutter but also all the genuine small contacts in the vicinity. The anti-clutter can be dangerous in the hands of the inexperienced. If in doubt, it is best left turned right down or off.

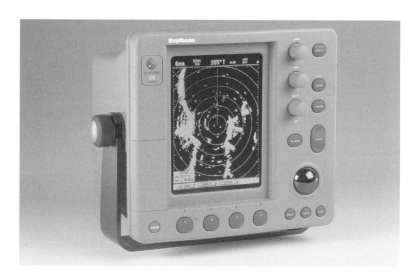

The controls on this Raytheon CRT display are very straight forward and easy to use.

RAIN CLUTTER   You might imagine that rain clutter on a radar screen would cause a similar image to sea clutter, but it doesn't. Rain certainly will reflect microwaves but, because a cloud of rain is less tangible than a solid object, its reflections will not have the crisp edge that you might expect from a large ship or tall cliff and the echo will tend to be less sharp and much longer. Consequently a rain cloud image on a radar screen appears fluffy, just like cotton wool (see right). The denser the rain cloud or shower, the more pronounced the image on the screen. Radar can therefore be

Rain clutter.

used to determine the track of heavy rain, showers and associated squalls. This facility is very useful to sailors seeking to avoid particularly unsettled weather. However, the radar is fitted with an **ANTI-CLUTTER** or **RAIN CLUTTER** control which will reduce the intensity of the image of rain clouds and heavy showers. Whilst this will also, to a lesser extent, reduce the echoes of other genuine contacts, the circuitry works differently from the sea clutter control so its effect is not so marked. However it still needs to be used with some caution.

INTERFERENCE REJECTION

INTERFERENCE REJECTION (IR) is an option on some sets to reduce the interference caused by nearby powerful radars. You may see a series of dots emanating from the centre of the screen in a series of spirals (see right) this indicates interference from another set. By using the IR setting, this interference will be reduced. Interference rejection does not have any other detrimental effects on the radar image and can therefore be left set.

Interference from another radar.

ECHO
STRETCH

ECHO STRETCH is designed to enhance the image size of weaker echoes to make them more conspicuous. However, it also enlarges the images of all echoes so that the crisp edge of land, which you might be using as an aid to pilotage, may still look crisp, but its real edge and the edge in the image will inevitably be different. You should be aware that narrow entrances to harbours can easily disappear if echo stretch is used as the reflections from each side overlap each other.

Echo stretch off; harbour
entrance is visible.

Echo stretch on; the entrance
appears to disappear.

ECHO TRAILS

ECHO TRAILS are traces on the screen recording the previous positions of radar contacts over a preset period of time. The time is usually optional, with a choice of changes over the previous 30 seconds or 1, 3, 6 and 12 minutes. There may be even an infinity (∞) option (ie all traces since the **ECHO TRAIL** facility was originally turned on are shown). The disadvantage with using **ECHO TRAIL** when there is an appreciable amount of land on the screen is that, over a period of time, it will 'wipe' a band across the screen which may obscure weak contacts. What it does provide though, is a good indication of the relative movements of other vessels. Take a look at Chapter 6 which covers collision avoidance and shows how the **ECHO TRAIL** facility can be a particularly useful tool if used carefully.

Echo trails.

BEARING DISCRIMINA-TION

In Chapter 2 we looked at horizontal beam widths and learned how it is preferable to select a set with a narrower beam width because the narrower the beam width, the more accurate the directional information will be, even though it will require a wider antenna to achieve it. A wide beam (see below) will not be able to differentiate between two contacts that are close together.

At a range of just over a mile, a radar with a 5° horizontal beam width would not be able to discriminate between two contacts 200 yards apart. A set with a narrower horizontal beam width of 2° (see below) could see between them at up to almost three miles.

Every reflected pulse that a radar with a 5° horizontal beam width receives back draws an image with an effective width of 5° on the screen. This explains why the entrance to a narrow harbour (about 200 yards wide) shows up as a solid image (without any sort of gap) on a radar screen with a 5° horizontal beam width. The gap only starts to show when you are within about a mile of it. Another of life's little boating mysteries explained.

SIDELOBES

The other factor to take into account when thinking about beam width is the weak pulses, called *sidelobes*, which

Having a radar antenna installed does not mean that you can dispense with a radar reflector. You may be able to see them but they have to be able to see you.

Main Pulse

emanate from the antenna either side of the main pulse.

These may affect the radar picture if a large contact passes close by. The sidelobes, instead of fading away, may actually be reflected back, causing a disturbed picture.

A contact passing close to port is shown on this screen (right). Extra reflections either side of the contact have been caused by the reflection of the sidelobes. This can be quite alarming the first time you see it on the screen, as it looks like a rather sinister contact stretching its arms out around you.

*RANGE
DISCRIMINA-
TION*

Most course books assert that radar is brilliant at measuring distance, and they are right up to a point. However it is important to understand that the range discrimination of a radar is dependent on the pulse length in use, which is, in turn, usually automatically determined by the selected range. Some radar sets may have an optional *long-pulse/short-pulse* switch but, in the main, the pulse length is likely to be automatically selected with the range scale.

A short microwave pulse of perhaps 0.08 micro-seconds (used on ranges up to say 1nm) will actually be about 24m in length. This means that as the radar transmitter fires the pulse, the leading edge of it will have travelled 24m before the rear edge leaves the antenna. However, in the case of a long microwave pulse of 1.2 micro-seconds (used on ranges from, say, 24nm), the length is around 360m. Thus a short pulse is much more effective at discriminating between two contacts in line less than 180m apart.

In the illustration below, the tail-end of the long pulse has not been reflected by the nearer vessel before the leading edge of the reflection from the same pulse off the further vessel has overtaken it on its way back.

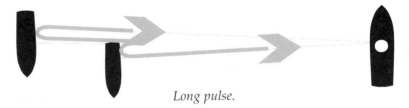

Long pulse.

The images on the radar screen will therefore merge and indicate just one contact.

If we now change to a lower range, and hence a shorter pulse length, the pulse reflected by the nearer vessel is on its way back to the antenna before the rest of the same pulse has even reached the further vessel (see below). Therefore the image on the screen will show as two separate contacts.

This explains why, at short range, the radar image becomes much more precise because of the shorter pulse lengths.

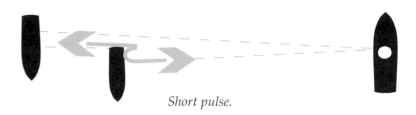

Short pulse.

SUPER-
REFRACTION

Another phenomenon that can affect the range of a radar is called *super-refraction*. We saw in Chapter 2 that the radar horizon is further away than the optical horizon because the atmosphere refracts (bends) microwaves slightly more than light. Common sense therefore dictates that if it is 'super', then the refraction must be greater than usual, causing the radar horizon to be extended further.

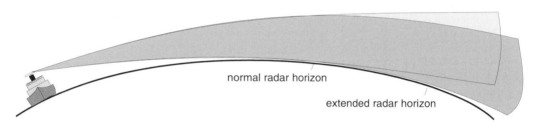

normal radar horizon

extended radar horizon

Super-refraction tends to be associated with a temperature inversion (where the temperature increases with height) or a hydrolapse (when humidity decreases with height). It is a summer phenomenon and is common (occurring at least once a week) in the southern North Sea and the English Channel and throughout the Mediterranean as well as off West Africa, the Arabian Sea, the Bay of Bengal and Sri Lanka. Super-refraction can increase the radar detection range by 15 – 20 per cent. There is no indication that super-refraction is happening unless you are comparing ranges received from the radar with ranges measured by other means such as regular fixing or plotter information.

DUCTING

Ducting is an exaggerated form of super-refraction caused by moist air on the surface of the sea being overrun by a layer of very dry warm air. It is not very common but is usually to be found on the lee side of hot land masses. Hence a southerly breeze in the Mediterranean may result in ducting, as hot air from the Sahara Desert blows over the moist surface of the sea. The refractive layer associated with ducting is normally less than 20m high.

SUB-REFRACTION

As super-refraction increases the radar detection range, so *sub-refraction* reduces it. Sub-refraction is caused by cool wind blowing over a warm sea. It is particularly associated with the warm sector of a depression and areas of the Arctic and Antarctic where cold offshore winds blow over a relatively warmer sea surface.

BLIND ARCS

Blind arcs are areas of radar 'blindness' caused by obstructions on the boat that prevent the passing of some of the microwave pulses from the antenna. A radar can only provide an effective image if it does not have any blind arcs or you are fully aware of any that do exist. This is why you will often see radar antennae mounted offset from the centreline on sailing boats so that the view directly ahead is not obscured by the mast.

Blind arcs on a ketch with mast-mounted radome.

Of course, the thing to remember is that, if your antenna is offset, there is almost certainly some area of your radar image which will still be obscured. If the width of the obstruction is less than half the horizontal beam width of the pulse, it should not present an enormous problem. Rigging rarely needs to be considered, but masts (especially when the radar antenna is mounted on a bracket in front of the mast), funnels, chimneys and other pieces of conspicuous superstructure can produce blind arcs.

To check for blind arcs, find a nice, solid, vertical harbour wall and set your range to the minimum setting. Slowly rotate the boat at rest just within the radar range you have set, watching the image of the wall. If part of its image starts to weaken or even break up as you slowly pivot the boat, note the relative bearing on which it is happening, stop the evolution and have a look from the antenna along the relative bearing to discover what is causing the obstruction. If the radar image of the wall actually parts, then there is a substantial obstruction. This could prove awkward because if another vessel were to close on you from that direction, it is unlikely that it would register on your radar screen.

RADAR SHADOWING

Radar shadowing occurs because radar cannot see through solid objects or around corners. Therefore, if a conspicuous object reflects back a series of radar pulses, the screen image will suggest that there is nothing beyond it (see below).

Vessel A will remain unseen by the radar as it is 'shadowed' by vessel B.

Radar shadowing also affects the images produced from reflections off coastlines (see diagram on page 32). A high foreground will totally obscure the lower lying areas behind, and promontories may totally alter the expected radar image.

In addition, the difference between the level of high and low water on gently sloping beaches can make a considerable difference to apparent distances on the radar screen (see diagram on page 32). If you plan to use the edge of a piece of land as a radar reference point, try to find a good steep cliff rather than a gently sloping sandy beach.

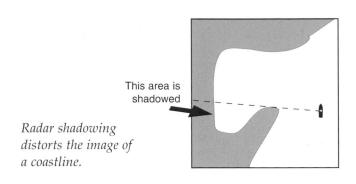

*Radar shadowing
distorts the image of
a coastline.*

This area is
shadowed

high water

low water

MEASURING BEARINGS & DISTANCES

The measurement of bearings and distances is probably the easiest task a radar operator can do. Bearings are measured using an *electronic bearing line* (**EBL**) which is usually hatched or dotted to differentiate it from the ship's heading marker. The **EBL** starts in the centre of the screen and emanates outwards to the outer edge. The **EBL** can be adjusted by moving it from side to side. A read-out underneath gives its bearing relative to the vessel's heading (up to 180° to port or starboard). If the radar is receiving heading information, it may be set to read in magnetic or even true bearings.

EBL

Range rings.　　　　　*Variable range marker.*　　　　　*Cross hairs.*

Generally, distances can be measured in three ways. Range rings (see above left) indicate a series of distances from the centre of the screen (your position). The distance between them changes according to the range scale in use. Distances in between the range rings have to be interpolated.

The *variable range marker* **VRM** is effectively a controllable range ring which can be expanded or contracted (see centre above). When correctly adjusted it gives a range reading in the panel beneath the screen.

Combined distance and bearing is available on some sets by a cross-hair symbol controlled on the screen by a roller ball or touch-sensitive pad (above right). The relative, magnetic or true bearing, together with the range at the position indicated by the cross hairs, is displayed beneath the screen.

HEAD-UP

In all the examples so far, the heading marker has been vertical from the centre of the screen upwards. This indicates that we are in the centre of the screen and we are heading upwards. Everything on the right of the screen is to starboard, everything on the left is to port, and anything in the bottom part of the screen is astern or behind us.

In 99 per cent of all small-craft radar sets this is the way that the radar is operated. It is known as **HEAD-UP** because the heading of the vessel is always up the screen. However, it is not the only option. Its obvious advantage is that the inexperienced operator can be confident that straight ahead is always pointing up the screen. The disadvantage is that any slight wanderings by the helmsman (and let's face it, it is impossible to steer a perfectly straight course) cause contacts on the screen to move around, making ranges and bearings much more difficult to measure. Fortunately, there is a way of stopping contacts on the screen from appearing to move around. Read on.

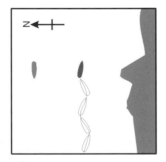

Operating head-up. Slight wanderings cause distortion of contacts.

NORTH-UP

Without any doubt whatsoever, **NORTH-UP** is the real answer to enthusiastic radar use. No, I'm serious. Why does every merchant ship and warship use its radar continuously set to **NORTH-UP**? It's true. It is not because professional seamen are more clever than you or I, it is because it really is

The advantage of north-up display is that it is orientated the same way as the chart.

the easiest way to operate. The only thing you have to come to terms with is the fact that the heading marker moves around instead of remaining static and pointing up the screen.

Don't give up hope at this stage – it does take a little bit of getting used to but consider the advantages:

1 The chart is orientated the same way as the radar picture. It is much easier to understand and distinguish land on the screen against that on the chart.
2 The contacts on the screen are 'stabilised'. That is to say, they don't move around with the vagaries of the helmsman.
3 You can see instantly on the screen which way your helmsman or autopilot is steering from the direction of the heading marker, without having to keep looking outside.

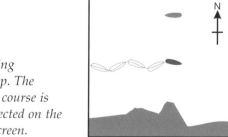

Operating north-up. The uneven course is not reflected on the radar screen.

Everyone should at least try using a radar in **NORTH-UP** mode if their set allows it. The main requirement is a heading input, which can normally be supplied from the fluxgate compass that drives the autopilot. It is technically possible to take heading information from a GPS but unfortunately a GPS's ability to assess direction if you stop moving or move very slowly is negligible, so this is not recommended.

COURSE-UP

COURSE-UP can be described as a 'half-way house'. If you practice waypoint navigation and use an autopilot to drive you from waypoint to waypoint, then selecting the **COURSE-UP** mode will stabilise the picture with the selected planned track pointing up the screen. This stabilises the movement of any contacts on the screen but still leaves everything showing on the screen to the right out on your starboard side and everything on the left to port etc. If you are more adventurous, don't stop at the half-way house: go the whole hog and go **NORTH-UP**, you'll love it!

A NOTE OF CAUTION

You have probably noted by now that I am a great advocate of using radar in **NORTH-UP** mode. You should be warned, however, that it is not good practice to swap backwards and forwards between **HEAD-UP** and **NORTH-UP**. If you like the concept of **NORTH-UP** (and I'm sure you will), don't keep swapping modes otherwise you will find that it is very easy to forget which mode you are in and get in a real pickle by misinterpreting the screen. If you're going to join the club, stay loyal to it.

TRUE MOTION

As the name **TRUE MOTION** suggests, the screen portrays the land as static and all the contacts on the screen, including your own vessel, move around in real time. To the layman this might seem ideal, and certain advantages are clear but there are pros and cons:

- All contacts moving on the screen are easily distinguishable, particularly if you use the **ECHO TRAIL** facility.

- All contacts which are stationary remain motionless on the screen regardless of whether your vessel is moving or not. On a *Relative* motion display (see Chapter 7), all stationary objects move across the screen at your speed in the opposite direction.

The disadvantages of *True* motion:

- Contacts closing on a steady bearing are not nearly as obvious as in *Relative* motion mode.
- The radar needs precise information about your vessel's speed through the water and its speed over the ground in order to correctly ascertain any drift or leeway whilst compiling the image.
- Every time the image is reset (which it has to be when you approach the edge of the screen) it upsets your concentration. It takes time to reassess a developing situation.

On a true motion display the land is static and the contacts, including your boat, move on the screen.

7 • Collision Avoidance

THE STEADY BEARING

Anyone who has spent any serious time at sea, or who has completed a navigation course, will know that in order to determine whether a risk of collision exists, you line up any visible vessel with one of your guardrails and see if it continues to stay in line with it. If it does, or it almost does, a risk of collision is said to exist. A more sophisticated way is to take a bearing of another vessel and if the bearing remains the same or nearly the same, again there is a risk of collision. Incidentally, it doesn't matter whether it's a true, magnetic or compass bearing. Providing your vessel's course doesn't change appreciably and you don't move the compass around the boat (affecting its deviation), this method works.

The question is can radar help in establishing whether a risk of collision exists? It certainly can, but before seeing how, it is important to understand relative motion.

RELATIVE MOTION

The majority of small radars work in what is called *Relative motion*. The radar has no idea whether your boat is moving or not. All it can establish is whether the contacts it picks up are moving relatively to the left or relatively to the right, getting relatively closer or relatively further away. This may not seem much help, but in terms of anti-collision work, that's exactly what you do need to know.

Let's go back to the concept of lining up a vessel you can see with one of the guardrails. What you are actually looking for is a change in her relative bearing. Is she moving relatively to the left of the guardrail or is she moving relatively to the right? If she remains in line with it, or nearly in line with it, there is a risk of collision provided, of course, the distance between you is decreasing.

Transferring this concept onto our simple radar screen, if we pick up a contact 45° on our starboard bow, five miles away, we could activate the movable hatched line – the electronic bearing line **EBL** – and swing it round into line with the contact. The radar screen would look like this. We are in the centre of the screen heading in the direction of the solid straight line (our heading marker). The contact which has now appeared is 45° to the right of the heading marker on our **EBL**. It is on the edge of the fifth ring out from the centre. On the six mile range, each ring indicates 1nm. We are therefore 5nm from the contact.

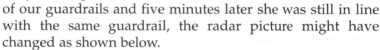

If, at the same time, we visually lined up the vessel with one of our guardrails and five minutes later she was still in line with the same guardrail, the radar picture might have changed as shown below.

The contact is now 3nm distant. However, the important thing is that she is still on the **EBL**. This indicates that she is still on the same relative bearing and that there is most definitely a risk of collision.

Now if we had been able to remember where she was ten minutes ago, we could more easily determine the real situation. This is the basis of using radar as an aid to collision avoidance.

Some years ago the keen navigator would have used a chinagraph pencil (sometimes called a grease pencil) to put a cross on the radar screen as soon as any contact appeared, and then another cross every three minutes or so. A straight line joining these crosses gave a good indication of

the movement of all contacts relative to his position in the centre of the screen. Any lines which, when extended, passed through the centre of the screen, indicated that a risk of collision existed. If subsequent crosses were put on the screen at the same time, then the different distances between them gave an indication of the relative speed that each vessel was moving. In the diagram at the bottom of page 39, vessel A will pass safely to port almost 2nm away but vessel B is definitely closing on a collision course.

More recently, an electronic means of leaving a trail behind each contact has become available, known as **ECHO TRACE** or **TRAILS**. Each contact leaves a continuous feint trail of its previous position over a preset period of time. The trace indicates the relative direction from which it has been travelling. This is then easily projected forward to assess the risk of collision. The length of the trace gives an indication of the relative speed.

In the diagrams below, the contacts A, B and C indicate moving contacts and D is land. Assuming that we are moving, A will pass safely to port and is on a reciprocal course to ours. B is on a heading to the left of ours at much the same speed and is alarmingly on a collision course, but note that she is not actually heading towards us.

 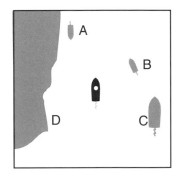

Trails facility in use.

C is overtaking us on a similar course to ourselves and the land D is moving down the screen as we effectively move up it. Note the broad trace which the land leaves behind it.

Do not use the **TRAILS** facility continuously for long periods otherwise the whole screen can easily become 'traced' over by large land masses and any small contacts may be lost in the trace.

PLOTTING

In the example on page 40, we saw that although the radar image indicated that B was coming towards us relatively, in fact the course she was steering was quite different. It is useful to know how to work out the true course and the speed of another vessel which we track on the radar. To do this you need to create a plotting sheet, which can simply be a plain piece of paper or use a copy of the blank plotting sheet shown in Appendix 5.

Range 5 miles on a relative bearing to starboard by 45° at 10:15.

Before any plotting can take place we need to know our course and speed. Let's assume we are travelling north at 18 knots. We need to note the relative bearing and distance of the contact of interest and make a note of the time. Let's say 45° to starboard (or green 45 for the more technically minded) at a range of 5nm at 10:15. Then after a measured period of time (say 10 minutes) we note the relative bearing and range of the contact again together with the time: still 45° to starboard but now at 3nm at 10.25. Because the relative bearing has remained constant, we know that a risk of collision exists. Our

Range 3 miles on the same relative bearing at 10:25.

course and speed have remained the same, namely north at 18 knots. Now we have sufficient information to plot the course and speed of the other vessel.

Take a copy of the plotting sheet on page 82, or, start off by drawing a vertical and a horizontal line which meet in the centre of a piece of paper and devise your own measuring scale. If you have a Breton plotter, keep it handy for measuring angles. Draw on the course that we are steering, in this case north. Draw the shape of the boat in the centre if it makes it clearer, pointing north.

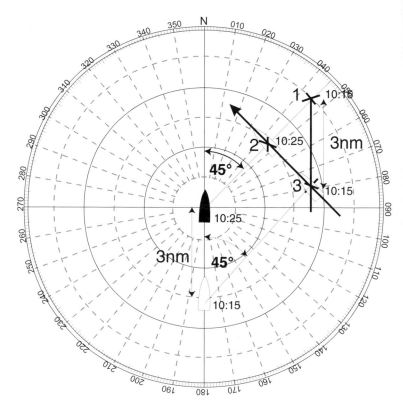

Example of the use of a plotting sheet to determine the actual heading of another vessel detected by radar alone in restricted visibility.

Using a suitable scale, mark off the distance at which you first recorded the contact – 5nm – and mark it on the paper 45° to the right of the boat's heading. This is shown by the cross marked **1**.

During the following 10 minutes, we know that our contact has moved relative to us from **1** to **2** and during the same time we have travelled 3nm north.

Just imagine that we had dropped a fender overboard at 10:15. Where would it be at 10:25? Answer: 3nm astern. So the contact we are monitoring would have been *relatively* 3nm astern of where it is now. That means that the position at which our contact was at 10:15 was 3nm down the screen (in the opposite direction to the way we are travelling) from position **1**, ie in position **3**.

So if position **3** is where it was 10 minutes ago, and position **2** is where it is now, it must actually be heading in the

A radar screen is integrated into this neat, efficient dashboard of the fly-bridge of a large motor yacht.

direction from position **3** to position **2**. Her speed is easily calculated from the plotting sheet by measuring the distance from **3** to **2** in a period of 10 minutes. In this example about 2nm in 10 minutes which equates to a speed of 12 knots.

I can remember spending hours and hours practising radar plotting as a student, but to be honest, I don't think I've ever done it for real since. If you are still lost, don't worry, your most important consideration in collision avoidance must always be the way contacts move *relatively* to you, not their true directional movement. True movement should only be of general interest.

CLOSEST POINT OF APPROACH (CPA)

The expression *closest point of approach* (CPA) is fairly self-explanatory, and using radar is the easiest way to establish how close another vessel is going to pass. As we discovered whilst plotting a contact earlier in this chapter, a vessel's relative heading and its true heading may be very different, so it is easy to be lulled into a false sense of security. The CPA is the closest that it will pass to you or you to it and is easily measured, either by plotting its progress across the screen using a chinagraph pencil, or by using the **ECHO TRAILS** facility. You either draw a line through the centre of the chinagraph plots or extend the echo's trail ahead of it. The CPA is the closest that the extended line comes to the centre of the screen and is easily measured using the range rings, a variable range marker (**VRM**) or a cursor.

In the illustration (right) we have been marking contact B every three minutes for the past 23 minutes and contact A for the past 11 minutes. The differing distance between the crosses indicates that the relative speed of B is much slower than the relative speed of A. By projecting the lines joining the crosses for each contact, the CPA can be seen as the tangent from each line which passes through the centre. In this case, contact A is actually at the CPA of 3nm on our port beam and the CPA of contact B will be 2nm on our starboard quarter, but not for some time.

TIME OF CLOSEST POINT OF APPROACH (TCPA)

It may be that you want to know how long it will be before a radar contact reaches its CPA. The *time of closest point of approach (TCPA)* is easy to calculate by noting the time that each cross is put on the screen and projecting the time forward (see diagram right). More sophisticated sets will calculate the TCPA automatically.

GUARD ZONES

Many radar sets are supplied with a *guard zone* facility which will activate an alarm if a radar contact comes within a predetermined area. These are usually, but not exclusively, set up using the electronic bearing line (**EBL**) and the variable

range marker (**VRM**) to set the
area over which the radar is to
keep watch. The radar can be set
to activate an alarm when a
contact comes within a specified
range of your vessel. Alternatively,
you can keep watch in a certain
area by setting the radar to sound
the alarm when a contact enters
that area. If the radar set is orientated to **HEAD-UP** then the area
selected will be relative to the

A sectored guard zone.

direction in which you are travelling at any time but if the
radar is set to **NORTH-UP** then the area covered can be the
true or magnetic bearings (according to the way the radar is
set up) and ranges from your position. It is important to
understand these differences.

Guard zones are particularly useful on passages in quiet
waters when, from time to time, your attention could stray. If
any contact comes within your preset zone, the alarm will
attract your attention.

Similarly, if you anchor in a
quiet cove, you may choose to use
an all-round guard zone which
will warn you if you are dragging
your anchor towards the shore. If
any piece of shoreline enters the
predetermined zone, an alarm
sounds. The problem with this is
that if the anchorage which you
have chosen is very busy, the
movement of every target into
your preset zone will activate the
alarm. This may become irritating.

All-round guard zone.

Certain radar sets allow for a variety of guard zones to be
set. However, these sophisticated variations are outside the
scope of this publication. If you own a radar set with other
guard zone options, you are referred to the owner's hand-
book, where they will be clearly described.

Automatic radar plotting (ARPA) helps the operator by tracking contacts which are considered hazardous and drawing a relative speed and direction vector for each one.

AUTOMATIC RADAR PLOTTING AID (ARPA)

The idea of creating a collision-avoiding radar is brilliant. The automatic radar plotting aid (ARPA) concept removes many of the difficulties faced by poorly trained watchkeepers in determining whether a potential collision situation is developing. The technology has been so successful that all merchant vessels over 300 tonnes are now obliged to be fitted with an ARPA radar as standard. The automatic plotting facility is now available on some small-craft radar sets, and, although it is not quite as sophisticated, it still does a super job.

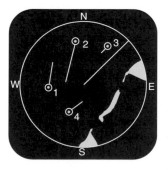

The ARPA concept is to track those contacts on the screen that are within a certain range and of a sufficient strength of signal to be considered a potential hazard. It ignores contacts which it calculates to be stationary. For each contact it selects, after a period of about a minute or so it draws a relative speed and direction vector and shows the position of that contact at a given time (chosen by the operator) in the future. Each contact is numbered or lettered and any contact may be selected by its reference using a joystick or tracker ball. Details are provided of its bearing and distance from you, its individual course, speed, CPA and TCPA. This information will appear on the console beneath the screen. In addition, an alarm will sound warning of any very dangerous contacts and any contacts which the radar was tracking and has unexpectedly lost. This is of enormous help to the bridge watchkeeper on a merchant ship, and is of equal assistance to the serious cruising yachtsman.

The ARPA facility is now available as an extra with many of the more sophisticated small-craft radar sets. The additional cost is modest and is certainly money well spent.

POSITION-FIXING USING RADAR

If you have undergone any sort of formal navigation training, you will know the textbook way of establishing your position. This recommends using a hand-bearing compass to take three bearings, ideally about 60° apart and to plot them on the chart providing a fix. However, success is not guaranteed, and you can end up with a 'cocked hat' or area of uncertainty.

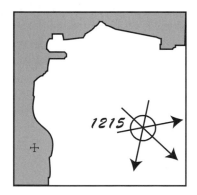

Textbook fix.

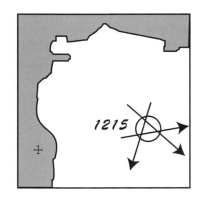

'Cocked hat'.

We established earlier in the book that radar is not completely reliable for taking bearings because of its horizontal beam width and the inaccuracy of the helmsman in steering a straight course. What we also discovered was that radar is excellent for measuring distances. With a bit of lateral thought, we can therefore establish our position using radar by taking the range or distance of three radar-conspicuous objects and plotting them in exactly the same way. The advantage of using a radar is that the inaccuracies associated with using a hand-bearing compass (deviation in particular) do not affect a radar fix. The principle is exactly the same.

Find three marks that are conspicuous to the radar. Remember that church spires and large buildings that you

Using radar to measure direction from conspicious objects can make your position-fixing more accurate than using a hand-bearing compass.

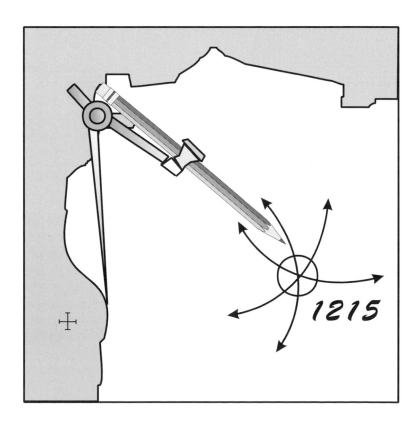

Radar fix.

can see will not be visible to the radar, whereas piers, irregular coastlines and steep cliffs are ideal. Instead of plotting the distances with a plotter, you need a pair of compasses. Instead of drawing a straight line from the point of interest, draw arcs with an arrow on each end to indicate a radar range. Don't forget to write the time alongside or the fix will be useless. If you are confident that the bearings which your radar outputs are accurate, or as accurate as you can achieve using a hand-bearing compass, there is no reason why a combined radar bearing and distance could not be used. However, always take two bearings and one range, or one range and two bearings, so that there is a built-in safety check.

COASTAL NAVIGATION USING RADAR

The radar can also be a very helpful aid in coastal navigation. It can, for example, ensure that you are always a certain minimum distance from a point or coastline. By using the variable range marker (**VRM**) to determine a set range, you can easily see whether you are too close or too far away from a recognised point. In the example shown, the radar can ensure that we are never closer than 3nm to the shore.

Establishing a minimum distance from shore.

Radar can be used to establish an anchorage at a predetermined distance from a radar-conspicuous object. Work out how far away you want to stop to lower the anchor. Let's say you decide on 1.7nm from a pier that is known to be conspicuous.

Set the **VRM** at that range and drive the boat towards the pier while watching its image move down the screen towards the edge

Establishing an anchorage at a predetermined distance.

of the **VRM**. Once it touches the **VRM** you are at the correct range, but don't forget to slow the boat right down just before you get there!

*ANCHORING
IN A PRE-
DETERMINED
POSITION*

If you want to anchor in a precise, predetermined position, rather than just a certain distance off, the radar makes life really easy. This is particularly so if your radar will allow you to set the image to **NORTH-UP** mode. Let's take the pier we used in the last example. But this time not only do we want to stop 1.7nm from the end of the pier, we also want it to bear 045° from us when we get there. Set the

*Anchoring in a precise
bearing: north-up mode.*

radar mode button to **NORTH-UP** or NU. Adjust the **EBL** to point in the required direction (ie 045°). Increase or reduce the reading of the **VRM** until it reads 1.7nm. Where the **VRM** and the **EBL** now cross is the position that you need to get the end of the pier to. The skill is in manoeuvring the boat so that you effectively 'drive' the end of the pier down your **EBL** until it touches the **VRM**, by which time you should have stopped.

What you have to remember is that to get the end of the pier to move to the right, you have to drive the boat to the left and vice versa. To get the pier closer to the **VRM**, you need to drive the boat towards the pier. If the pier ends up inside the **VRM**, then you have gone too far and you need to back away or turn round. Turning round won't interfere with the radar image because, being **NORTH-UP** the picture is sta-bilised. By turning round, all that will happen is that the heading marker will swing round indicating your heading, but the pier will remain in the same place on the screen.

Once you have tried this, you will realise just how quick and easy finding a particular point using radar actually is. All you need is to know the range and bearing of a radar-conspicuous mark from the anchorage position of your choice. It is a good technique to use whether or not the visibility is bad, and it will certainly get you just where you plan to be without any fuss or bother.

RACON

The radar transponder (**RACON**) or the radar transponder beacon (**RA**dar bea**CON**) enables the navigator to identify various specific navigation marks. The **RACON** on the mark is activated by the pulse of a nearby vessel, and sends back an encoded Morse letter a fraction of a second behind its own echo. This appears on the radar screen as an extended dash or series of

RACON marks use Morse as identifying codes.

dot(s) and/or dash(es) (taken from the Morse Code) on the screen starting at the position of the navigation mark and extending outwards from the centre. On the chart above it is shown as **RACON** or **RACON (T)** indicating its characteristic as being simply a dash (Morse Code for T). As the system has become more popular, more distinguishing characteristics were required, so several Morse letters are now used to differentiate between marks. **RACON (K)**, for example is a dash, a dot and a dash (Morse Code for K). In order to conserve its own power and not continuously obliterate an area of the screen, the **RACON** will usually only react about every third or fourth sweep of your radar aerial. Who said that the Morse Code was no longer any use to seafarers?

SART

Similar in terms of the way it works to a **RACON**, a **SART** (or Search And Rescue Transponder) is also able to indicate its position on a radar screen. However it is not used in conjunction with navigation marks but as a rescue aid. **SART**s are either fitted on deck in float-free mountings or packed as part of the equipment included in

The initial radar image of an active SART.

a liferaft. A **SART** should be taken by the crew when abandoning ship. However, if it is left behind, it will float free should the vessel sink before it is removed. Like the **RACON**, it responds to radar pulses with its own characteristic series of 12 dots on an X-Band radar screen. It is used to alert vessels in the vicinity that there is an emergency and it guides potential rescuers towards the rescue scene.

The **SART** is powered by a 6-volt lithium battery which is designed to last for six years before requiring replacement and will operate the transponder for up to 96 hours in standby mode, and more than eight hours in active mode. **SART**s are an important part of the worldwide Global Maritime Distress and Safety System (GMDSS) which is now compulsory on vessels over 300 tons. **SART** signals will show up on

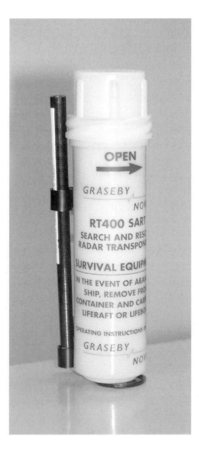

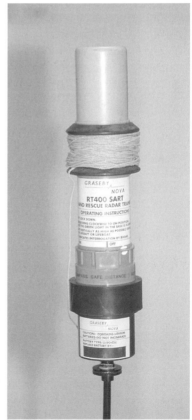

Left: a SART (Search and Rescue Transponder) in its waterproof container and (right) ready for action.

the radar screens of all vessels at ranges of up to eight miles. Once the potential rescuer gets within a mile, the 12 dots change to concentric rings, indicating that the casualty is near. At the same time an audible alarm and/or flashing light is activated on the **SART** itself to indicate to the casualties that help is at hand.

The radar image of an active SART at close range.

9 • Blind Pilotage

To the professional mariner, the expression 'blind pilotage' is part of his everyday vocabulary. However to many small-craft users, the idea of trying to comprehend the blind pilotage concept seems too difficult.

This is a great shame as blind pilotage is an excellent method of navigation in coastal and confined waters, particularly if your screen orientation is able to be set to **NORTH-UP** and your set will allow you to draw offset electronic bearing lines (**EBL**s) or *parallel indices* (see below). This is the way the professionals navigate and if it works for them, it will certainly work for you.

If your set will not allow **NORTH-UP** and will not allow offset **EBL**s do not give up hope. It is possible to use the principle of parallel indexing on a **HEAD-UP** set, but you will be very dependent upon the accuracy of your helmsman's steering. If you cannot draw offset **EBL**s don't despair, as the offset **EBL** facility can be emulated by using string and Blu-Tack. I'm not joking, it really does work.

PARALLEL INDEX (PI) TECHNIQUES

Using a parallel index (**PI**) is easy. There are two simple stages:

- Draw the planned track(s) that you wish to follow onto the chart (Fig 9.1, page 56). Let's suppose we want to travel from bottom left of the chart shown opposite, around the west cardinal buoy, and then off to the east.
- Read off the bearing of each track and identify the point of closest proximity to a radar-conspicuous edge of land or object. To do this, draw a line parallel to the planned track that skirts the edge of a radar-conspicuous coastline or object. Then measure the perpendicular distance and note whether it is offset to the left or the right of your planned track (Fig 9.2, page 57).

In Fig 9.2 the first planned track of 010° is conveniently

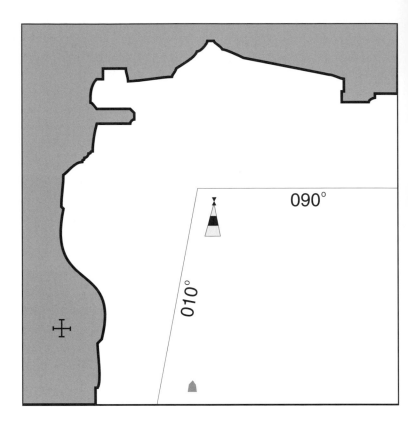

Fig 9.1 Draw the planned track onto the chart.

close to a curved length of coastline A, which will show clearly on the radar screen. Another track could be extended to run through the end of the pier B which is equally conspicuous. On the next course, the square-ended jetty C looks as if it will show clearly, so another line is drawn parallel to the second planned track, and so on. Then the important measurements to take are the perpendicular distances between each planned track and the parallel line through the conspicuous marks. The parallel index (or **PI**) is the line which is drawn parallel to the planned track and the distance between them is the offset to the left or right of the track you intend to follow.

This can be simply tabulated in a notebook as follows:

1st Course	010°	offset left by 1.2nm
Alternative 1st Course	010°	offset left by 1.4nm
2nd Course	090°	offset left by 1.6nm

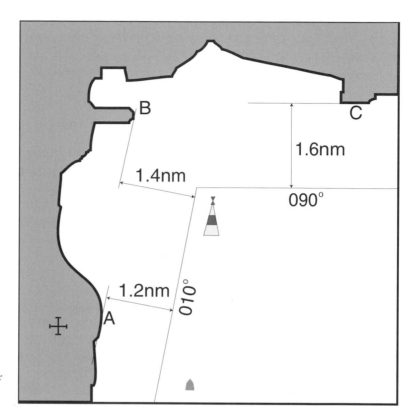

Fig 9.2 Measure the perpendicular distance and note whether it is offset to the left or right of your planned track.

This information should now be transferred to the radar screen. There are a number of different methods of drawing lines on radar screens. If your radar set has offset electronic bearing lines (**EBL**s) or a facility for parallel indices (**PI**) then use one of those. If not, do not despair, as a piece of fine string or cotton thread stuck to the edge of the screen with Blu-Tack or a similar sticky substance will more than adequately do the job. Trust me, it works.

Three parallel index lines.

*CONDUCTING
A COASTAL
PASSAGE
USING RADAR*

Having set up the radar screen, we can now consider how the radar can keep us on the track we have planned. In our example, Fig 9.2, we know that we want the radar image of curved shoreline to align with the 010° offset port 1.2nm line, and the end of the pier to line up on the 010° offset port 1.4nm line. The skill is to drive the boat so that the radar images line up. Once they are lined up, you are on the planned track. As the boat proceeds in the direction 010°, the images of the curved land and the pier remain on their respec-

Stage 1: Steer so that the curved shore line aligns with the right hand of the two vertical parallel index lines.

tive lines. If they start to move away you must respond. Remember that if the land image gets too far away, steer towards the land, and if it gets too close then steer away. With a little practice, coastal navigation could not be simpler.

The interesting thing to consider is that providing the selected radar image remains moving down its chosen line, then the course you actually steer to keep the image on the line will automatically take into account the effects of wind and tide. If you like, it provides an automatic means of working out a course to steer.

Stage 2: The pier continues to align with the left hand of the two vertical parallel index lines.

You may wonder what happens when you come to a course alteration. Going back to our example, once we have passed the west cardinal buoy on our starboard side, we plan to alter to starboard to a new course of 090°.

We shall need to have completed the turn by the time the square-ended jetty comes into line with the third line which we drew. Because boats take time to alter course we need to start our alteration, say 200 yards or so before the jetty lines up. That will allow enough time for the turn to get under way and be completed just as the square jetty comes into line. Any number of alterations can be pre-planned but it is advisable to restrict the number of lines on your screen to two or three as a maximum, or the screen will become cluttered. It is very easy to misinterpret a contact against the wrong line with potentially disastrous results.

It may be that your aim is not to steer along a specific track but, instead, to keep a certain distance away from a conspicuous mark. The same technique can be used to achieve this end.

Radar plays a prominent role for Sea Start, the marine equivalent of the AA, in their search and assist operations.

Stage 3: By the time the square-ended jetty aligns with the horizontal parallel index lines, the alteration of course should be completed.

Firstly, draw a straight line through a radar-conspicuous coastline, parallel to the direction in which you intend to travel. Decide on the closest safe distance to the line which you will be content to travel (see Fig 9.3). Draw a second line parallel to the first. (This becomes in effect the clearing line which you do not wish to cross.)

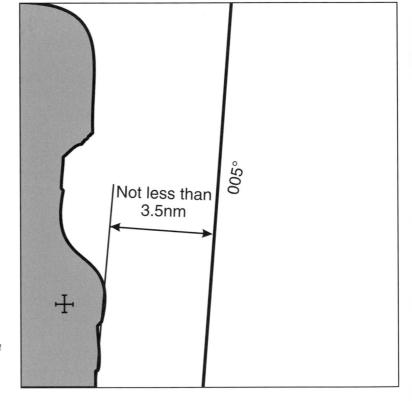

Fig 9.3. Decide on the closest safe distance to the line of travel and draw a second line parallel to the first.

With the radar in **NORTH-UP** mode, set the **EBL** in the direction of the two parallel lines and offset the **EBL** by the distance measured.

As long as the land to the left of the clearing line remains to the left of it, you can be certain that you are more than 3.5nm away from the coastline.

Coastal navigation and pilotage using radar is remarkably straightforward once you understand the principle of blind pilotage. Remember, virtually all professional seamen prefer this means of navigation if they are given a choice.

It seems odd to me, therefore, that amateurs, who have radar sets quite capable of coping with a stabilised screen and drawing lines, rarely actually try it out. Why not give it a go and discover an entirely new navigation technique?

A single clearing line.

10 • Integration with Other Navigation Aids

RADAR AND WAYPOINT NAVIGATION

Electronic navigation equipment is manufactured to a standard agreed by the National Marine Electronics Association (NMEA) in March 1983. The NMEA 0183 standard comprises one-way communication between a single output and multiple repeaters. This was considered more than adequate at the time it was introduced, but as technology has moved on and more and more electronic equipment has become available, each with its own message to tell, this one-way communication has proved restrictive.

A new standard, known as NMEA 2000, will be introduced in 2000, comprising a low cost, bi-directional, multi-transmitter, multi-receiver serial data network. This will have a capacity approximately 20 times that of the NMEA 0183 and should enable a wider interchange of information than is possible at present.

That is not to say that current radars cannot interface with Global Positioning Systems (GPS), chart plotters and autopilots using NMEA 0183; they can and do.

Modern radar sets can easily interface with GPS sets and other electronic instruments.

Probably the most useful integration between a plotter, radar and autopilot is when navigating using waypoints. The first stage is to programme the GPS or plotter with the intended route. The route is made up of a series of waypoints entered in the order which you wish to pass them (usually by their latitude and longitude). They can also be entered direct from the chart display on a plotter.

If you choose the position of buoys as waypoints, take great care because your autopilot does not understand how significant a buoy can be. If you instruct the autopilot to head towards the buoy and drive straight into it you will almost certainly do far more damage to your vessel than you will do to the buoy!

Once the waypoints are loaded into the GPS or plotter's memory, they form a route. The autopilot can be set to follow the route from waypoint to waypoint, sounding an audible alarm as the boat approaches each one.

The position of the waypoint is displayed on the radar screen in the form of a 'lollipop' (see right). At the same time it is common for the range and bearing of the next waypoint, together with the 'time to go' (TTG) to the next waypoint to be displayed adjacent to the screen. This gives you an easy answer to that question, endlessly repeated by the younger members

of the crew, 'Are we there yet?' If you do choose to use buoys as waypoints, the lollipop will draw your attention to the position of the buoy as you approach and should sound an audible alarm once you are getting close.

You should be aware that if you choose the waypoint method of electronic navigation, the autopilot will steer to keep the boat on the straight line between the selected way-points, so it will continually correct for the effects of wind, tide or current. The practical effect is that you will rarely seem to be pointing towards the next waypoint until you are getting quite close. The other point to note is that you will not be travelling the shortest distance.

If you wish to take the quickest route, then you should calculate the course to steer in the old fashioned way using vector triangles (any book on navigation will explain) and set the autopilot course accordingly.

**RADAR
AND CHART
PLOTTERS
COMBINED**

It is possible to combine the radar display and plotter display in one unit. This is undoubtedly a great advantage for those with restricted space but it does come with a warning. If your set can alternate between the radar picture and the chart picture, then take great care that you know which one you are looking at! If you are able to split the screen so that the radar picture is in the top half of the screen with the chart image in the bottom part (or side by side), that is unlikely to cause confusion. With the alternating screen it is very easy to mistake the chart for the radar picture when you have had a long day, it's rough, dark and miserable and you are, to put it mildly, overtired. I have seen an experienced (though exhausted) watchkeeper looking at the plotter picture and heard him say, 'It's quiet out there tonight.'

It is very handy to be able to combine radar display with the chart plotter.

Equipment is now available (though at a high price) that will overlay an electronic chart with a transparent radar image. Thus those radar images which originate from charted objects should coincide. Any that don't are therefore worthy of closer inspection.

This facility is a great step forward in navigational technology and certainly worth close inspection at the next boat show you visit.

The benefits of radar are little understood and as a result it is underused. If this book has cast new light on radar's value as an aid to navigation and cruising safety, it has more than fulfilled its purpose.

Appendix 1 • Radar Bands

You may hear a radar described as 'such and such' a band. This harps back to the early development of radar during World War II. Whilst this will be of little concern to the cruising yachtsman, for those closet anoraks whose lives would not be complete without knowing more about the different types of radar frequencies and wavelengths, prepare yourself for a real treat!

C-BAND   4GHz–8GHz, 4cm–8cm wavelength. Used for short range surveillance particularly of weather around airports.

K-BAND   12GHz–18GHz and 27GHz–40GHz, 1.7cm–2.5cm and 0.75cm –1.2cm wavelength. Actually two separate bands split down the middle by a strong water vapour absorption line. Used for very short-range surveillance.

L-BAND   1GHz–2GHz, 15cm–30cm wavelength. Used in longer-range weather studies but requires considerable power.

S-BAND   2GHz–4GHz, 8cm–15cm wavelength. Used in long-range surveillance but requires a large scanner and considerable power.

X-BAND   8GHz–12GHz, 2.5cm–4.0cm wavelength. The usual small craft and small-ship navigation radar. Relatively short range, but not requiring huge amounts of power.

Appendix 2 • Calculation of Radar Horizon and Maximum Range

The geometric horizon in nautical miles is calculated:
1.92 x √height of eye in metres

The optical horizon in nautical miles is calculated:
2.08 x √height of eye in metres

The radar horizon in nautical miles is calculated:
2.23 x √height of radar antenna in metres

The effective radar range of a high shoreline in nautical miles is calculated as follows:
2.23 x (√radar antenna height in metres + √shoreline height in metres)

Extracts from the International Regulations on the Prevention of Collisions at Sea are provided below, including the rules covering reduced visibility and the use of radar.

RULE 5: LOOK-OUT

Every vessel shall at all times maintain a proper look-out by sight and hearing as well as by all available means appropriate in the prevailing circumstances and conditions so as to make a full appraisal of the situation and of the risk of collision.

RULE 6: SAFE SPEED

Every vessel shall at all times proceed at a safe speed so that she can take proper and effective action to avoid collision and be stopped within a distance appropriate to the prevailing circumstances and conditions. In determining a safe speed the following factors shall be among those taken into account:

(a) By all vessels:
- (i) the state of visibility;
- (ii) the traffic density including concentrations of fishing vessels or any other vessels;
- (iii) the manoeuvrability of the vessel with special reference to stopping distance and turning ability in the prevailing conditions;
- (iv) at night, the presence of background light such as from shore lights or from back scatter of her own lights;
- (v) the state of wind, sea and current, and the proximity of navigational hazards;

(b) Additionally, by vessels with operational radar:
- (i) the characteristics, efficiency and limitations of the radar equipment;

(ii)   any constraints imposed by the radar range scale in use;

(iii) the effect on radar detection of the sea state, weather and other sources of interference;

(iv)   the possibility that small vessels, ice and other floating objects may not be detected by radar at an adequate range;

(v)   the number, location and movement of vessels detected by radar;

(vi)   the more exact assessment of the visibility that may be possible when radar is used to determine the range of vessels or other objects in the vicinity.

RULE 7: RISK OF COLLISION

(a) Every vessel shall use all available means appropriate to the prevailing circumstances and conditions to determine if risk of collision exists. If there is any doubt, such risk shall be deemed to exist.

(b) Proper use shall be made of radar equipment if fitted and operational, including long-range scanning to obtain early warning of risk of collision and radar plotting or equivalent systematic observation of detected objects.

(c) Assumptions shall not be made on the basis of scanty information, especially scanty radar information.

(d) In determining if risk of collision exists, the following considerations shall be among those taken into account:

(i)   such risk shall be deemed to exist if the compass bearing of an approaching vessel does not appreciably change;

(ii)   such risk may sometimes exist even when an appreciable bearing change is evident, particularly when approaching a very large vessel or a tow, or when approaching a vessel at close range.

RULE 8: ACTION TO AVOID COLLISION

(a) Any action taken to avoid collision shall, if the circumstances of the case admit, be positive, made in ample time and with due regard to the observance of good seamanship.

(b) Any alteration of course and/or speed to avoid collision shall, if the circumstances of the case admit, be large enough to be readily apparent to another vessel observing visually or by radar: a succession of small alterations of course and/or speed should be avoided.

(c) If there is sufficient sea room, alteration of course alone may be the most effective action to avoid a close-quarters situation provided that it is made in good time, is substantial, and does not result in another close-quarters situation.

(d) Action taken to avoid collision with another vessel shall be such as to result in passing at a safe distance.

The effectiveness of the action shall be carefully checked until the other vessel is finally past and clear.

(e) If necessary to avoid collision or allow more time to assess the situation, a vessel shall slacken her speed or take all way off by stopping or reversing her means of propulsion.

(f)(i)   A vessel which, by any of these Rules, is required not to impede the passage or safe passage of another vessel shall, when required by the circumstances of the case, take early action to allow sufficient sea room for the safe passage of the other vessel.

(ii)   A vessel required not to impede the passage or safe passage of another vessel is not relieved of this obligation if approaching the other vessel so as to involve risk of collision and shall, when taking action, have full regard to the action which may be required by the Rules of this part.

(iii)   A vessel the passage of which is not to be impeded remains fully obliged to comply with the Rules of this part when the two vessels are approaching one another so as to involve risk of collision.

RULE 19:
CONDUCT OF
VESSELS IN
RESTRICTED
VISIBILITY

(a) This Rule applies to vessels not in sight of one another when navigating in or near an area of restricted visibility.

(b) Every vessel shall proceed at a safe speed adapted to the prevailing circumstances and conditions of restricted visibility.

A power-driven vessel shall have her engines ready for immediate manoeuvre.

(c) Every vessel shall have due regard to the prevailing circumstances and conditions of restricted visibility when complying with the Rules of Section 1 of this Part.

(d) A vessel which detects by radar alone the presence of another vessel shall determine if a close-quarters situation is developing and/or risk of collision exists.

If so, she shall take avoiding action in ample time, provided that when such action consists of an alteration of course, so far as possible the following shall be avoided:

(i)   an alteration of course to port for a vessel forward of the beam, other than for a vessel being overtaken;

(ii) an alteration of course towards a vessel abeam or abaft the beam.

(e) Except where it has been determined that a risk of collision does not exist, every vessel which hears apparently forward of her beam the fog signal of another vessel, or which cannot avoid a close-quarters situation with another vessel forward of her beam, shall reduce her speed to the minimum at which she can be kept on her course.

She shall if necessary take all her way off and in any event navigate with extreme caution until danger of collision is over.

RULE 32:
DEFINITIONS

(a) The word 'whistle' means any sound-signalling appliance capable of producing the prescribed blasts and which complies with the specifications in Annex III to these Regulations.

(b) The term 'short blast' means a blast of about one second's duration.

(c) The term 'prolonged blast' means a blast of from four to six seconds' duration.

RULE 33:
EQUIPMENT
FOR SOUND
SIGNALS

(a) A vessel of 12 metres or more in length shall be provided with a whistle and a bell and a vessel of 100 metres or more in length shall, in addition, be provided with a gong, the tone and sound of which cannot be confused with that of the bell.

The whistle, bell and gong shall comply with the specifications in Annex III to these Regulations.

The bell or gong or both may be replaced by other equipment having the same respective sound characteristics, provided that manual sounding of the prescribed signals shall always be possible.

(b) A vessel of less than 12 metres in length shall not be obliged to carry the sound signalling appliances prescribed in paragraph **(a)** of the Rule but if she does not, she shall be provided with some other means of making an efficient sound signal.

RULE 35:
SOUND
SIGNALS IN
RESTRICTED
VISIBILITY

In or near an area of restricted visibility, whether by day or night, the signals prescribed in this Rule shall be used as follows:

(a) A power-driven vessel making way through the water shall sound at intervals of not more than 2 minutes, one prolonged blast.

(b) A power-driven vessel under way but stopped and making no way through the water shall sound at intervals of not more than 2 minutes two prolonged blasts in succession with an interval of about 2 seconds between them.

(c) A vessel not under command, a vessel restricted in her ability to manoeuvre, a vessel constrained by her draught, a sailing vessel, a vessel engaged in fishing and a vessel engaged in towing or pushing another vessel shall, instead of the signals prescribed in paragraphs **(a)** or **(b)** of this Rule, sound at intervals of not more than 2 minutes three blasts in succession, namely one prolonged followed by two short blasts.

(d) A vessel engaged in fishing, when at anchor, and a vessel restricted in her ability to manoeuvre when carrying out her work at anchor, shall instead of the signals prescribed in paragraph **(g)** of this Rule sound the signal prescribed in paragraph **(c)** of this Rule.

(e) A vessel towed or if more than one vessel is towed the last vessel of the tow, if manned, shall at intervals of not more than 2 minutes sound four blasts in succession, namely one prolonged followed by three short blasts.

When practicable, this signal shall be made immediately after the signal made by the towing vessel.

(f) When a pushing vessel and a vessel being pushed ahead are rigidly connected in a composite unit they shall be regarded as a power-driven vessel and shall give the signals prescribed in paragraphs **(a)** or **(b)** of this Rule.

(g) A vessel at anchor shall at intervals of not more than one minute ring the bell rapidly for about 5 seconds.

In a vessel of 100 metres or more in length the bell shall be sounded in the forepart of the vessel and immediately after the ringing of the bell the gong shall be sounded rapidly for about 5 seconds in the after part of the vessel.

A vessel at anchor may in addition sound three blasts in succession, namely one short, one prolonged and one short blast, to give warning of her position and of the possibility of collision to an approaching vessel.

(h) A vessel aground shall give the bell signal and if required the gong signal prescribed in paragraph **(g)** of this Rule and shall, in addition, give three separate and distinct strokes on the bell immediately before and after the rapid ringing of the bell.

A vessel aground may in addition sound an appropriate whistle signal.

(i) A vessel of less than 12 metres in length shall not be obliged to give the above-mentioned signals but, if she does not, shall make some other efficient sound signal at intervals of not more than 2 minutes.

(j) A pilot vessel when engaged on pilotage duty may in addition to the signals prescribed in paragraphs **(a)**, **(b)** or **(g)** of this Rule sound an identity signal consisting of four short blasts.

COMMENTS ON THE INTERNA- TIONAL REGULATIONS

- You should note that if your vessel is fitted with an operational radar, you *shall* use it. [*Rule 7(b)*.]
- You *shall* maintain a proper look out by all means available. This includes radar. [*Rule 5*.]
- If there is any doubt as to whether a risk of collision exists, you *shall* assume that one does and act accordingly. [*Rule 7(a)*.]
- You *shall* not make assumptions on scanty information, especially scanty radar information [*Rule 7(c)*.]
- If you give way to another vessel, your alteration *shall* be sufficiently bold as to be easily detected by another vessel both visually and, more importantly, by its radar operator. [*Rule 8(b)*.]

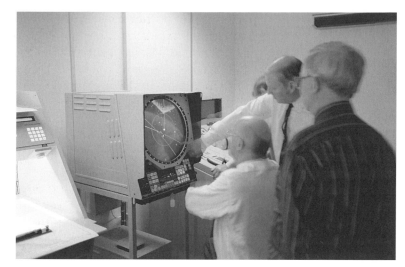

If you are still unsure whether using radar is for you, an RYA radar training course will almost certainly turn you into a convert.

- Vessels navigating in restricted visibility should note that the rules change fundamentally. There is no stand-on vessel in fog. All vessels effectively become give-way vessels and if you detect another vessel by radar alone, you should avoid an alteration to port for a vessel forward of the beam, and avoid an alteration towards a vessel which is abeam or abaft the beam. [*Rule 19(d)*.]
- Before you decide to anchor in fog remember that some poor unsuspecting soul is required to ring your ship's bell for 5 seconds every minute. This task is not designed for improving your crew's morale especially if it remains foggy for a long time. [*Rule 35(g)*.]

Amplification Increasing the amplitude of a radio wave to increase its power.

Analogue An older type of radar display.

Beam width The width of a radar beam, or more precisely, the angle through which the power of the radar signal is at least 50 per cent of its maximum power.

Blind arc An area shielded from radar transmissions, and therefore from radar reception also, usually by part of the ship's structure, mast(s), funnel(s) or rigging.

Brilliance A control which regulates the brightness of the radar picture.

Cathode ray tube (CRT) The component which creates the radar picture.

Chinagraph A pencil with greasy lead which used to be used for making plotting marks on radar screens. It is sometimes called a grease pencil.

Closest point of approach (CPA) The point at which an approaching vessel will be closest to your own.

Cocked hat The triangle formed by the intersection of three position lines giving an indication of the accuracy of a fix. The smaller the cocked hat, the better the accuracy.

Compass course Refers to a direction defined using a magnetic compass before it is corrected for deviation and variation.

Compass safe distance The minimum distance from a compass at which a piece of electrical equipment should be installed without causing a deviation of more than 1°.

Contact The bright blob on a radar screen which represents the position of a radar-reflective object which is often referred to as a target.

Course The direction in which a vessel is intended to move through the water – not necessarily the same as its track or heading.

Course-up display Describes a radar display in which the picture is stabilised so that the vessel's intended course is straight up the screen.

CPA Closest point of approach.

Cursor An electronically generated marker used to indicate a position on a raster-scan display. It can also mean the line in the centre on the rotating grid of index lines normally associated with an analogue display.

Deviaton A compass error affecting magnetic compasses caused by the vessel's own magnetic field.

Differentiation Another name for the rain clutter circuit.

Discrimination A radar set's ability to show targets which are close to each other as separate contacts.

Drift The rate at which a boat moves due to the effect of current or tidal stream.

Ducting A natural phenomenon causing an exaggerated form of super-refraction resulting in a greatly extended radar range.

Echo The returning radar signal reflected from a target or radar contact. Also referred to as a contact.

Echo stretch A facility to enhance weaker signals. Care must be taken if the radar is being used for pilotage as the image becomes distorted.

Echo trails The means of recording the relative movement of radar contacts over a predetermined period of time.

Electronic bearing line (EBL) An electronically produced line radiating from the centre of the screen which can be rotated around the screen to assist in taking bearings or assessing potential close-quarters situations.

Estimated position (EP) A vessel's calculated position, taking into account its course and speed together with the effects of wind and tide or current.

Fix A vessel's known position at a particular time.

Gain See amplification.

Global Positioning System (GPS) A satellite navigation system offering worldwide position fixing with an accuracy usually within about 200m.

Grease pencil See chinagraph.

Guard zone An area of the radar screen defined by the operator, within which the presence of a radar contact causes an audible alarm to sound.

Head-up display A radar display mode in which the vessel's heading is straight up the screen and the picture is unstabilised.

Heading The direction in which the vessel is pointing at any moment.

Heading mark A straight bright line on a radar screen representing the vessel's heading. It is fixed, pointing up the screen in head-up mode but moves from side to side of the upright in course-up mode or it points in the direction that a vessel is heading in north-up mode.

Hertz, Heinrich Rudolph German physicist (1857–94) who gave his name to the unit of radio frequency or cycle per second. Early pioneer of what was to become radar technology.

Horizontal beam width The width of the beam of a radar measured horizontally.

Interfacing Connecting two or more electronic navigation aids together so that information can be passed from one to the other.

Interference rejection A facility to remove interference from nearby radars on other vessels. It does not have any other detrimental effect upon the image and can be left set on.

Leeway A vessel's sideways movement through the water caused by the wind.

Liquid Crystal Diode (LCD) An electronic component whose colour can be made to change by stimulating it with a voltage. Banks of liquid crystal diodes can be connected together to form a display.

Magnetic course Describes directions relative to magnetic north. Differs from true by an error known as variation, an error induced by the earth's magnetic field.

Magnetron An electronic valve which uses a powerful permanent magnet to produce pulses of microwaves.

Microsecond One millionth of a second.

Microwaves Electromagnetic waves whose wavelength and frequency are between those of radio waves and infrared.

NMEA The National Marine Electronics Association – an American organisation responsible for defining most of the standard interfaces used in marine electronics. The most common one is NMEA 0183 but will be replaced by NMEA 2000.

Noise Random electromagnetic interference appearing on a radar screen as tiny dots.

North-up display A radar display mode in which the picture is stabilised by a compass input so that north is stabilised at the top of the screen.

Open array antenna A radar whose aerial is not enclosed within a cover or radome. Also referred to as an open scanner.

Open scanner See open array antenna.

Optical horizon The maximum distance seen by the naked eye along the earth's surface at sea level.

Pixel A picture cell. One of many thousands of tiny squares which join together to make up the picture on a raster-scan radar.

Plan position indicator (PPI) The most common type of radar display format, in which contacts appear in the form of a map or plan.

Plotting A system of observing and recording the movement of radar contacts to establish their actual course and speed from their relative motion.

Plotting sheet Paper forms used to transfer relative movement into true movement.

Pulse A very short transmission of radio waves or microwaves.

Pulse length The duration of a pulse.

Pulse repetition frequency (PRF) The number of pulses per second.

Quantized Describes a radar display in which each pixel can appear at a variety of several levels of colour.

RACON A RAdar BeaCON: a device fitted to important navigation marks which transmits its own signal when stimulated by the transmission from a nearby radar set. Causes a distinctive flash on the radar screen which may be coded using Morse letters for easy recognition.

Radar Derives from the expression RAdio Direction And Ranging.

Radar horizon The maximum distance seen by a radar along the earth's surface at sea level.

Radar reflector A passive device designed to increase the strength of the echo produced by small craft or navigation marks.

Radome A rigid cover enclosing the radar aerial together with the transmitter and receiver circuitry.

Rain clutter Weaker contacts caused by radar echoes from low cloud, rain, snow or hail.

Range The distance between your own vessel and a contact, or the scale at which the radar has been set to operate.

Range rings Rings on the radar screen representing predetermined ranges used for measuring distance.

Raster-scan A type of radar display whose picture is produced in digital format showing the range and bearing of each contact, in the form of hundreds of thousands of pixels on the screen.

Resolution See discrimination.

S-Band Microwaves whose wavelength is in the order of 10cm. Mainly used in commercial ship radars.

SART Search and Rescue Transponder – required in the GMDSS Regulations as a safety aid designed to paint a series of 12 dots on the radar screens of vessels in the vicinity.

Scanner A rotating aerial; or the unit of which the aerial is a part.

Sea clutter Spurious contacts caused by radar echoes from waves.

Set The direction of movement of a current or tidal stream.

Shadow areas Areas shielded from radar transmissions by solid objects outside the vessel.

Sidelobes Radio energy propagated by the radar antenna outside its beam width.

Slotted wave guide A type of radar antenna made up of a length of precision-made metal tubing with a series of accurately milled slots in one side.

Standby When the radar is switched on and most of its systems are functioning, but the transmitter is not transmitting.

Strobe A range ring whose range can be varied by the operator.

Sub-refraction A natural phenomenon causing the radar range to be reduced.

Super-refraction A natural phenomenon causing the radar range to be extended.

Sweep A rotating radial line in the picture produced by an analogue radar, which is sometimes artificially simulated in raster-scan sets.

Target Any reflective object within the operating range of a radar set.

Track A vessel's movement relative to the ground.

Tracker ball A ball, built into the control panel of a radar set, and used to control the movement of a cursor.

Trails The means of recording the relative movement of radar contacts over a predetermined period of time.

Transmit (TX) When the radar is functioning fully and producing a display of the surrounding area in plan form on the PPI.

Transit Two or more objects which lie on the same bearing from an observer, ie which appear in line with each other.

True course Directions referred to true north, ie referred to a line joining the earth's north and south poles. Differs from magnetic north by a variable error known as variation, caused by the earth's magnetic field.

True motion A radar display which takes account of the transmitting vessel's own movement, so as to show the movement of each target including the transmitting vessel relative to the ground.

Tuning Adjustment of the radar receiver to maximise the reception of weak return echoes.

Vertical beam width The beam width of a radar pulse measured vertically.

Variable range marker (VRM) A range ring whose radius can be varied by the operator to help measure ranges accurately.

Wave guide A hollow metal duct, used to conduct microwaves within a radar set.

Williamson turn A method of turning a vessel under power to ensure that she returns down her wake. Often recommended for man overboard recovery. A predetermined amount of helm is applied until the heading is 60°–70° from the original course when the helm is reversed using the same amount of helm. When the boat has swung onto the reciprocal of the original course, she will be heading down her own wake and should enable a man overboard to be sighted easily.

X-Band Microwaves, with a wave length around 3cm, used in many marine radars and particularly in sets designed for small craft.

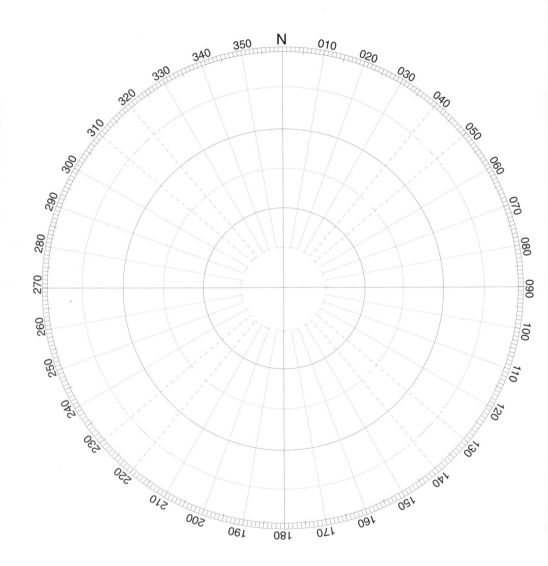

This page may be photocopied.

Index